50 Barbecue Recipes for the Holiday Season

By: Kelly Johnson

Table of Contents

- Maple-Glazed Barbecue Ribs
- Cranberry BBQ Turkey Breast
- Spiced Apple Cider Pork Chops
- Honey Mustard Grilled Chicken
- Smoky Holiday Beef Brisket
- Garlic Herb Lamb Skewers
- Balsamic-Glazed Grilled Vegetables
- Festive Pineapple Ham Steaks
- Bourbon BBQ Shrimp
- Pomegranate-Glazed Duck Breast
- Hickory-Smoked Pulled Pork
- Rosemary and Garlic Grilled Salmon
- Holiday Herb-Rubbed Chicken Wings
- Maple and Sage Pork Tenderloin
- Spicy Christmas Chili Grilled Steak
- Peppermint BBQ Lamb Chops
- Sweet and Spicy BBQ Meatballs
- Orange-Glazed Grilled Duck
- Cherry BBQ Pork Ribs
- Mustard-Crusted Grilled Salmon
- Holiday-Style BBQ Vegetable Kebabs
- Applewood-Smoked Turkey Legs
- Festive BBQ Jackfruit (vegan)
- Grilled Holiday Sausage Platter
- Sweet Potato BBQ Skewers
- BBQ Glazed Holiday Ham
- Cinnamon and Clove BBQ Chicken Thighs
- Maple Bourbon Grilled Shrimp
- Grilled Holiday Stuffed Mushrooms
- Sweet Cranberry BBQ Chicken Drumsticks
- BBQ Pineapple and Bacon Skewers
- Maple BBQ Glazed Pork Belly
- Holiday Herb-Marinated Grilled Trout
- Festive BBQ Veggie Burgers
- Spicy BBQ Duck Legs

- Caramelized Onion BBQ Beef Burgers
- Grilled Eggplant and Zucchini Rolls
- BBQ Gingerbread-Spiced Ribs
- Holiday Citrus BBQ Chicken Breast
- Cranberry Balsamic Glazed Salmon
- Grilled Maple-Glazed Sweet Corn
- Smoked BBQ Chestnuts (vegan)
- Grilled Rosemary Lamb Kebabs
- Sweet Holiday BBQ Brisket Sandwiches
- Grilled Pear and Walnut Salad
- Cinnamon BBQ Pork Chops
- Pomegranate BBQ Glazed Chicken Wings
- Grilled Holiday Shrimp Skewers
- Spiced BBQ Holiday Meatloaf
- Hickory-Smoked BBQ Tofu (vegan)

Maple-Glazed Barbecue Ribs

Ingredients

- **For the Ribs:**
    - 2 racks of baby back ribs (about 4-5 lbs total)
    - 1 tablespoon salt
    - 1 teaspoon black pepper
    - 2 teaspoons smoked paprika
    - 1 teaspoon garlic powder
    - 1 teaspoon onion powder
    - 1 teaspoon chili powder
- **For the Maple Glaze:**
    - 1 cup pure maple syrup
    - 1/4 cup ketchup
    - 2 tablespoons apple cider vinegar
    - 2 tablespoons Dijon mustard
    - 1 tablespoon soy sauce
    - 1/2 teaspoon smoked paprika
    - 1/4 teaspoon cayenne pepper (optional, for heat)

Instructions

1. **Prepare the Ribs:**
    - Remove the thin membrane from the back of the ribs.
    - In a small bowl, mix salt, black pepper, smoked paprika, garlic powder, onion powder, and chili powder.
    - Rub the spice mixture generously over both sides of the ribs.
    - Cover the ribs and refrigerate for at least 2 hours, or overnight for maximum flavor.
2. **Cook the Ribs (Oven Method):**
    - Preheat the oven to 275°F (135°C).
    - Wrap each rack of ribs tightly in aluminum foil and place them on a baking sheet.
    - Bake for 2.5–3 hours, or until the ribs are tender and the meat is pulling away from the bones.
3. **Prepare the Maple Glaze:**
    - In a small saucepan over medium heat, combine maple syrup, ketchup, apple cider vinegar, Dijon mustard, soy sauce, smoked paprika, and cayenne pepper (if using).

- Bring the mixture to a simmer and cook for 5–7 minutes, stirring occasionally, until slightly thickened. Remove from heat.
4. **Grill and Glaze:**
   - Preheat your grill to medium heat.
   - Remove the ribs from the foil and place them on the grill, bone side down.
   - Brush the ribs generously with the maple glaze. Grill for 5–10 minutes, turning occasionally and basting with more glaze, until caramelized and lightly charred.
5. **Serve:**
   - Remove ribs from the grill, let rest for 5 minutes, and slice into portions.
   - Serve with extra glaze on the side if desired.

Cranberry BBQ Turkey Breast

Ingredients

- 1 boneless turkey breast (about 2 lbs)
- 1 cup cranberry sauce (homemade or canned)
- 1/2 cup barbecue sauce
- 1 tablespoon apple cider vinegar
- 1 teaspoon smoked paprika
- 1/2 teaspoon garlic powder
- Salt and pepper to taste

Instructions

1. Preheat oven to 375°F (190°C).
2. Mix cranberry sauce, barbecue sauce, apple cider vinegar, smoked paprika, and garlic powder in a bowl.
3. Season turkey breast with salt and pepper. Place in a baking dish and pour half the cranberry BBQ sauce over it.
4. Bake for 1–1.5 hours, basting with additional sauce every 20 minutes, until the internal temperature reaches 165°F (74°C).
5. Let rest for 10 minutes before slicing. Serve with remaining sauce.

Spiced Apple Cider Pork Chops

Ingredients

- 4 bone-in pork chops
- 1 cup apple cider
- 1 tablespoon apple cider vinegar
- 2 tablespoons brown sugar
- 1/2 teaspoon cinnamon
- 1/4 teaspoon nutmeg
- 1/4 teaspoon cloves
- 1 tablespoon olive oil
- Salt and pepper to taste

Instructions

1. Season pork chops with salt and pepper.
2. Heat olive oil in a skillet over medium heat. Sear pork chops for 2–3 minutes on each side until browned.
3. In a bowl, mix apple cider, vinegar, brown sugar, cinnamon, nutmeg, and cloves.
4. Pour mixture into the skillet, reduce heat to low, and simmer for 15–20 minutes, flipping chops occasionally, until cooked through (145°F or 63°C internal temperature).
5. Serve with pan sauce drizzled on top.

Honey Mustard Grilled Chicken

Ingredients

- 4 boneless, skinless chicken breasts
- 1/4 cup honey
- 1/4 cup Dijon mustard
- 1 tablespoon olive oil
- 1 tablespoon lemon juice
- 1 teaspoon garlic powder
- Salt and pepper to taste

Instructions

1. In a bowl, whisk together honey, Dijon mustard, olive oil, lemon juice, garlic powder, salt, and pepper. Reserve 1/4 cup for basting.
2. Place chicken breasts in a zip-top bag or shallow dish and pour remaining marinade over. Marinate in the refrigerator for at least 30 minutes or up to 2 hours.
3. Preheat grill to medium-high heat. Grill chicken for 6–7 minutes per side, basting with reserved marinade, until the internal temperature reaches 165°F (74°C).
4. Remove from grill, let rest for 5 minutes, and serve.

Smoky Holiday Beef Brisket

Ingredients

- 4–5 lbs beef brisket
- 2 tablespoons smoked paprika
- 1 tablespoon garlic powder
- 1 tablespoon onion powder
- 2 teaspoons salt
- 1 teaspoon black pepper
- 1/2 teaspoon cayenne pepper
- 1 cup beef broth
- 1 cup barbecue sauce
- 2 tablespoons liquid smoke

Instructions

1. Preheat oven to 300°F (150°C).
2. Mix smoked paprika, garlic powder, onion powder, salt, black pepper, and cayenne pepper. Rub generously over the brisket.
3. Place brisket in a roasting pan, pour beef broth and liquid smoke around it, and cover tightly with foil.
4. Bake for 4–5 hours, until fork-tender. Remove foil, brush with barbecue sauce, and bake uncovered for 15 minutes.
5. Slice against the grain and serve.

Garlic Herb Lamb Skewers

Ingredients

- 2 lbs lamb shoulder or leg, cut into 1-inch cubes
- 1/4 cup olive oil
- 2 tablespoons fresh rosemary, chopped
- 1 tablespoon fresh thyme, chopped
- 4 cloves garlic, minced
- 1 teaspoon lemon zest
- Salt and pepper to taste

Instructions

1. In a bowl, mix olive oil, rosemary, thyme, garlic, lemon zest, salt, and pepper. Add lamb cubes and toss to coat. Marinate for 2 hours.
2. Preheat grill to medium-high heat. Thread lamb onto skewers.
3. Grill for 8–10 minutes, turning occasionally, until browned and cooked to your desired doneness.

Balsamic-Glazed Grilled Vegetables

Ingredients

- 1 zucchini, sliced
- 1 eggplant, sliced
- 1 red bell pepper, cut into strips
- 1 yellow squash, sliced
- 1/4 cup balsamic vinegar
- 2 tablespoons olive oil
- 1 tablespoon honey
- Salt and pepper to taste

Instructions

1. In a bowl, whisk balsamic vinegar, olive oil, honey, salt, and pepper. Toss vegetables in the mixture.
2. Preheat grill to medium heat. Grill vegetables for 3–5 minutes per side, brushing with glaze, until tender and caramelized.

Festive Pineapple Ham Steaks

Ingredients

- 4 ham steaks
- 1/4 cup brown sugar
- 1/4 cup pineapple juice
- 2 tablespoons Dijon mustard
- 1/4 teaspoon ground cloves

Instructions

1. In a small bowl, mix brown sugar, pineapple juice, Dijon mustard, and ground cloves.
2. Heat a skillet or grill pan over medium heat. Cook ham steaks for 3 minutes per side, brushing with glaze, until heated through and caramelized.

Bourbon BBQ Shrimp

Ingredients

- 1 lb large shrimp, peeled and deveined
- 1/4 cup bourbon
- 1/4 cup barbecue sauce
- 1 tablespoon brown sugar
- 1 tablespoon olive oil
- 1 teaspoon smoked paprika

Instructions

1. In a bowl, mix bourbon, barbecue sauce, brown sugar, olive oil, and smoked paprika. Toss shrimp in the marinade and let sit for 30 minutes.
2. Heat a grill or skillet over medium-high heat. Cook shrimp for 2–3 minutes per side until opaque.

Pomegranate-Glazed Duck Breast

Ingredients

- 2 duck breasts
- 1/2 cup pomegranate juice
- 2 tablespoons honey
- 1 teaspoon balsamic vinegar
- Salt and pepper to taste

Instructions

1. Score the duck skin in a crisscross pattern. Season with salt and pepper.
2. Heat a skillet over medium heat and cook duck skin-side down for 6–8 minutes. Flip and cook another 4–5 minutes.
3. In a saucepan, simmer pomegranate juice, honey, and balsamic vinegar until thickened. Brush over duck before serving.

Hickory-Smoked Pulled Pork

Ingredients

- 4–5 lbs pork shoulder
- 2 tablespoons smoked paprika
- 1 tablespoon garlic powder
- 1 tablespoon onion powder
- 1 teaspoon cayenne pepper
- 1 cup apple cider vinegar
- 1/4 cup brown sugar

Instructions

1. Rub pork shoulder with smoked paprika, garlic powder, onion powder, and cayenne pepper.
2. Place in a smoker at 225°F (107°C) and smoke for 6–8 hours, until internal temperature reaches 205°F (96°C).
3. Let rest, shred, and mix with apple cider vinegar and brown sugar mixture.

Rosemary and Garlic Grilled Salmon

Ingredients

- 4 salmon fillets
- 2 tablespoons olive oil
- 2 teaspoons fresh rosemary, chopped
- 2 cloves garlic, minced
- 1 tablespoon lemon juice
- Salt and pepper to taste

Instructions

1. In a bowl, mix olive oil, rosemary, garlic, lemon juice, salt, and pepper. Brush over salmon fillets.
2. Grill salmon over medium heat for 4–5 minutes per side, until opaque and flaky.

Holiday Herb-Rubbed Chicken Wings

Ingredients

- 2 lbs chicken wings
- 1 tablespoon olive oil
- 1 tablespoon fresh rosemary, chopped
- 1 tablespoon fresh thyme, chopped
- 1 teaspoon smoked paprika
- 1/2 teaspoon garlic powder
- Salt and pepper to taste

Instructions

1. Toss chicken wings with olive oil, rosemary, thyme, smoked paprika, garlic powder, salt, and pepper.
2. Preheat oven to 400°F (200°C). Arrange wings on a baking sheet and bake for 35–40 minutes, flipping halfway, until golden and crispy.

Maple and Sage Pork Tenderloin

Ingredients

- 2 pork tenderloins (about 1 lb each)
- 1/4 cup pure maple syrup
- 2 tablespoons Dijon mustard
- 1 tablespoon fresh sage, chopped
- 2 cloves garlic, minced
- Salt and pepper to taste

Instructions

1. Preheat oven to 400°F (200°C).
2. In a small bowl, whisk together maple syrup, Dijon mustard, sage, garlic, salt, and pepper.
3. Rub the pork tenderloins with the maple mixture.
4. Heat a skillet over medium-high heat and sear the tenderloins for 2–3 minutes per side.
5. Transfer the pork to the oven and roast for 20–25 minutes, until the internal temperature reaches 145°F (63°C).
6. Let rest for 5 minutes before slicing and serving.

Spicy Christmas Chili Grilled Steak

Ingredients

- 4 steaks (ribeye or flank)
- 2 tablespoons olive oil
- 1 tablespoon chili powder
- 1 teaspoon smoked paprika
- 1/2 teaspoon cayenne pepper
- 1 teaspoon garlic powder
- 1/2 teaspoon cumin
- Salt and pepper to taste

Instructions

1. Preheat grill to medium-high heat.
2. In a bowl, mix olive oil, chili powder, smoked paprika, cayenne pepper, garlic powder, cumin, salt, and pepper.
3. Rub the mixture evenly over both sides of the steaks.
4. Grill steaks for 4–6 minutes per side for medium-rare, or longer for desired doneness.
5. Let the steaks rest for 5 minutes before serving.

Peppermint BBQ Lamb Chops

Ingredients

- 8 lamb chops
- 1/4 cup fresh mint, chopped
- 2 tablespoons honey
- 2 tablespoons soy sauce
- 1 tablespoon balsamic vinegar
- 1/2 teaspoon ground ginger
- Salt and pepper to taste

Instructions

1. In a bowl, whisk together mint, honey, soy sauce, balsamic vinegar, ground ginger, salt, and pepper.
2. Coat lamb chops with the marinade and let them sit for at least 30 minutes.
3. Preheat grill to medium-high heat. Grill lamb chops for 4–5 minutes per side for medium-rare.
4. Rest for a few minutes before serving.

Sweet and Spicy BBQ Meatballs

Ingredients

- 1 lb ground beef or turkey
- 1/2 cup breadcrumbs
- 1/4 cup grated Parmesan cheese
- 1 egg
- 1/4 cup BBQ sauce
- 2 tablespoons honey
- 1 teaspoon hot sauce
- 1/2 teaspoon chili flakes
- Salt and pepper to taste

Instructions

1. Preheat oven to 375°F (190°C).
2. In a bowl, mix ground meat, breadcrumbs, Parmesan, egg, salt, and pepper. Shape into 1-inch meatballs.
3. Place meatballs on a baking sheet and bake for 15–20 minutes, until cooked through.
4. In a small saucepan, combine BBQ sauce, honey, hot sauce, chili flakes, and simmer for 5 minutes.
5. Toss meatballs in the sauce and serve.

Orange-Glazed Grilled Duck

Ingredients

- 2 duck breasts
- 1/2 cup fresh orange juice
- 1 tablespoon honey
- 2 tablespoons soy sauce
- 1/2 teaspoon ginger
- 1/2 teaspoon ground coriander
- Salt and pepper to taste

Instructions

1. Score the skin of the duck breasts and season with salt and pepper.
2. In a saucepan, combine orange juice, honey, soy sauce, ginger, and coriander. Simmer until thickened, about 10 minutes.
3. Preheat grill to medium heat. Grill duck, skin-side down, for 6–7 minutes. Flip and cook for another 4–5 minutes.
4. Brush the orange glaze over the duck during the last few minutes of grilling.
5. Rest for 5 minutes before slicing and serving.

Cherry BBQ Pork Ribs

Ingredients

- 2 racks baby back ribs
- 1 cup cherry preserves
- 1/4 cup BBQ sauce
- 1 tablespoon apple cider vinegar
- 1 teaspoon smoked paprika
- Salt and pepper to taste

Instructions

1. Preheat oven to 275°F (135°C).
2. Remove the thin membrane from the ribs. Season with salt, pepper, and smoked paprika.
3. In a bowl, mix cherry preserves, BBQ sauce, and apple cider vinegar.
4. Place ribs on a baking sheet, cover with foil, and bake for 2.5–3 hours.
5. Remove foil, brush with the cherry BBQ sauce, and grill or broil for an additional 10–15 minutes until caramelized.

Mustard-Crusted Grilled Salmon

Ingredients

- 4 salmon fillets
- 1/4 cup Dijon mustard
- 2 tablespoons brown sugar
- 1 tablespoon olive oil
- 1 tablespoon fresh dill, chopped
- Salt and pepper to taste

Instructions

1. In a small bowl, whisk together Dijon mustard, brown sugar, olive oil, dill, salt, and pepper.
2. Coat salmon fillets with the mustard mixture.
3. Preheat grill to medium-high heat. Grill salmon for 4–5 minutes per side, until cooked through.
4. Serve immediately.

Holiday-Style BBQ Vegetable Kebabs

Ingredients

- 1 zucchini, sliced
- 1 red bell pepper, cut into chunks
- 1 yellow bell pepper, cut into chunks
- 1 red onion, cut into wedges
- 8 oz mushrooms, whole or halved
- 2 tablespoons olive oil
- 1/4 cup balsamic vinegar
- 1 tablespoon honey
- 1 teaspoon dried oregano
- Salt and pepper to taste

Instructions

1. Preheat grill to medium heat.
2. In a bowl, whisk olive oil, balsamic vinegar, honey, oregano, salt, and pepper. Toss vegetables in the marinade.
3. Thread vegetables onto skewers.
4. Grill for 4–5 minutes per side, until tender and lightly charred.

Applewood-Smoked Turkey Legs

Ingredients

- 4 turkey legs
- 2 tablespoons olive oil
- 1 tablespoon smoked paprika
- 1 teaspoon garlic powder
- 1 teaspoon onion powder
- 1/2 teaspoon cayenne pepper
- Salt and pepper to taste

Instructions

1. Preheat smoker to 250°F (120°C).
2. Rub turkey legs with olive oil, smoked paprika, garlic powder, onion powder, cayenne pepper, salt, and pepper.
3. Smoke turkey legs for 2.5–3 hours, until internal temperature reaches 165°F (74°C).
4. Rest for 10 minutes before serving.

Festive BBQ Jackfruit (Vegan)

Ingredients

- 2 cans young green jackfruit in brine (drained and shredded)
- 1/2 cup BBQ sauce (vegan)
- 1 tablespoon olive oil
- 1 onion, sliced
- 2 cloves garlic, minced
- 1 teaspoon smoked paprika
- 1 teaspoon cumin
- 1/2 teaspoon chili powder
- Salt and pepper to taste
- 1 tablespoon fresh cilantro (optional, for garnish)

Instructions

1. In a large pan, heat olive oil over medium heat. Add the onions and garlic and sauté until softened, about 5 minutes.
2. Add the shredded jackfruit to the pan and cook for another 5 minutes.
3. Stir in the smoked paprika, cumin, chili powder, salt, and pepper, then add the BBQ sauce. Mix well to coat the jackfruit.
4. Simmer for 10–15 minutes, allowing the flavors to meld.
5. Serve the BBQ jackfruit on buns or as a side dish, garnished with fresh cilantro if desired.

Grilled Holiday Sausage Platter

Ingredients

- 6 vegan sausages (or traditional sausages)
- 1 tablespoon olive oil
- 1/2 teaspoon smoked paprika
- 1/2 teaspoon garlic powder
- Salt and pepper to taste
- Fresh parsley for garnish

Instructions

1. Preheat grill to medium-high heat.
2. Brush sausages with olive oil and sprinkle with smoked paprika, garlic powder, salt, and pepper.
3. Grill sausages for 6–8 minutes per side, or until golden and cooked through.
4. Serve sausages on a platter with fresh parsley for garnish.

Sweet Potato BBQ Skewers

Ingredients

- 2 medium sweet potatoes, peeled and cut into cubes
- 1 tablespoon olive oil
- 1/4 cup BBQ sauce
- 1 red bell pepper, cut into chunks
- 1 zucchini, sliced
- 1 red onion, cut into wedges
- Salt and pepper to taste

Instructions

1. Preheat grill to medium-high heat.
2. Toss sweet potato cubes in olive oil, salt, and pepper.
3. Thread sweet potatoes, bell pepper, zucchini, and onion onto skewers, alternating the veggies.
4. Grill skewers for 10–12 minutes, turning occasionally, until sweet potatoes are tender and veggies are lightly charred.
5. Brush with BBQ sauce during the last 2 minutes of grilling.

BBQ Glazed Holiday Ham

Ingredients

- 1 pre-cooked ham (about 4–5 lbs)
- 1/2 cup BBQ sauce
- 1/4 cup maple syrup
- 2 tablespoons Dijon mustard
- 1/2 teaspoon ground cinnamon
- 1/2 teaspoon ground cloves
- Salt and pepper to taste

Instructions

1. Preheat oven to 350°F (175°C).
2. In a bowl, whisk together BBQ sauce, maple syrup, Dijon mustard, cinnamon, cloves, salt, and pepper.
3. Place the ham in a roasting pan and brush with the BBQ glaze.
4. Roast the ham for 1.5–2 hours, basting with the glaze every 30 minutes.
5. Let the ham rest for 10 minutes before slicing and serving.

Cinnamon and Clove BBQ Chicken Thighs

Ingredients

- 6 bone-in, skin-on chicken thighs
- 2 tablespoons olive oil
- 1 tablespoon ground cinnamon
- 1 teaspoon ground cloves
- 1/4 cup BBQ sauce
- Salt and pepper to taste

Instructions

1. Preheat grill to medium-high heat.
2. Rub chicken thighs with olive oil, cinnamon, cloves, salt, and pepper.
3. Grill chicken thighs for 6–7 minutes per side, until the internal temperature reaches 165°F (74°C).
4. Brush with BBQ sauce during the last few minutes of grilling.
5. Let the chicken rest for 5 minutes before serving.

Maple Bourbon Grilled Shrimp

Ingredients

- 1 lb large shrimp, peeled and deveined
- 1/4 cup maple syrup
- 2 tablespoons bourbon
- 1 tablespoon soy sauce
- 1 teaspoon smoked paprika
- 1/2 teaspoon ground ginger
- Salt and pepper to taste

Instructions

1. In a bowl, mix maple syrup, bourbon, soy sauce, smoked paprika, ginger, salt, and pepper.
2. Toss shrimp in the marinade and refrigerate for 30 minutes.
3. Preheat grill to medium-high heat.
4. Thread shrimp onto skewers and grill for 2–3 minutes per side, until cooked through.
5. Serve immediately with extra marinade on the side.

Grilled Holiday Stuffed Mushrooms

Ingredients

- 12 large mushroom caps, stems removed
- 1/4 cup breadcrumbs
- 1/4 cup grated vegan cheese (or regular cheese)
- 1/4 cup chopped fresh parsley
- 2 cloves garlic, minced
- 1 tablespoon olive oil
- Salt and pepper to taste

Instructions

1. Preheat grill to medium heat.
2. In a bowl, combine breadcrumbs, cheese, parsley, garlic, olive oil, salt, and pepper.
3. Stuff the mushroom caps with the breadcrumb mixture.
4. Grill stuffed mushrooms for 5–7 minutes, until the mushrooms are tender and the topping is golden.
5. Serve immediately.

Sweet Cranberry BBQ Chicken Drumsticks

Ingredients

- 8 chicken drumsticks
- 1/4 cup cranberry sauce
- 1/4 cup BBQ sauce
- 1 tablespoon honey
- 1 tablespoon Dijon mustard
- Salt and pepper to taste

Instructions

1. Preheat grill to medium heat.
2. In a bowl, whisk together cranberry sauce, BBQ sauce, honey, Dijon mustard, salt, and pepper.
3. Season drumsticks with salt and pepper, then brush with the cranberry BBQ glaze.
4. Grill drumsticks for 25–30 minutes, turning occasionally and basting with the glaze.
5. Let the chicken rest for 5 minutes before serving.

BBQ Pineapple and Bacon Skewers

Ingredients

- 1 fresh pineapple, cut into chunks
- 8 slices bacon
- 1 tablespoon olive oil
- 1 tablespoon BBQ sauce
- Salt and pepper to taste

Instructions

1. Preheat grill to medium-high heat.
2. Cut bacon slices in half and wrap around pineapple chunks, securing with toothpicks.
3. Brush skewers with olive oil and BBQ sauce, then season with salt and pepper.
4. Grill skewers for 8–10 minutes, turning occasionally, until bacon is crispy and pineapple is caramelized.
5. Serve immediately.

Maple BBQ Glazed Pork Belly

Ingredients

- 2 lbs pork belly, skin scored
- 1/4 cup maple syrup
- 1/4 cup BBQ sauce
- 1 tablespoon soy sauce
- 1 tablespoon apple cider vinegar
- 1 teaspoon smoked paprika
- Salt and pepper to taste

Instructions

1. Preheat oven to 300°F (150°C).
2. In a bowl, whisk together maple syrup, BBQ sauce, soy sauce, apple cider vinegar, smoked paprika, salt, and pepper.
3. Rub the mixture over the pork belly, ensuring it's well-coated.
4. Place the pork belly on a rack in a roasting pan and bake for 2–2.5 hours, until tender.
5. Increase the temperature to 400°F (200°C) and bake for an additional 20–30 minutes to crisp up the skin.
6. Let the pork rest for 10 minutes before slicing and serving.

Holiday Herb-Marinated Grilled Trout

Ingredients

- 4 trout fillets, skin on
- 1/4 cup olive oil
- 2 tablespoons lemon juice
- 2 cloves garlic, minced
- 1 tablespoon fresh thyme, chopped
- 1 tablespoon fresh rosemary, chopped
- Salt and pepper to taste

Instructions

1. In a small bowl, whisk together olive oil, lemon juice, garlic, thyme, rosemary, salt, and pepper.
2. Place trout fillets in a shallow dish and pour the marinade over them. Refrigerate for 30 minutes.
3. Preheat grill to medium-high heat.
4. Grill trout fillets for 4–5 minutes per side, or until the fish is cooked through and flakes easily.
5. Serve immediately with extra lemon wedges.

Festive BBQ Veggie Burgers

Ingredients

- 2 cups cooked black beans, mashed
- 1/2 cup breadcrumbs
- 1/4 cup grated carrot
- 1/4 cup finely chopped red onion
- 1/4 cup chopped fresh parsley
- 2 tablespoons BBQ sauce
- 1 teaspoon smoked paprika
- Salt and pepper to taste

Instructions

1. In a large bowl, combine mashed black beans, breadcrumbs, carrot, red onion, parsley, BBQ sauce, smoked paprika, salt, and pepper.
2. Form the mixture into patties.
3. Preheat grill to medium heat.
4. Grill veggie burgers for 4–5 minutes per side, until golden and firm.
5. Serve on buns with your favorite toppings.

Spicy BBQ Duck Legs

Ingredients

- 4 duck legs
- 1/4 cup olive oil
- 1/4 cup BBQ sauce
- 2 tablespoons sriracha sauce
- 1 teaspoon ground cumin
- 1 teaspoon smoked paprika
- Salt and pepper to taste

Instructions

1. Preheat grill to medium heat.
2. In a bowl, mix together olive oil, BBQ sauce, sriracha sauce, cumin, paprika, salt, and pepper.
3. Rub the marinade over the duck legs and let them marinate for 30 minutes.
4. Grill duck legs for 8–10 minutes per side, until the skin is crispy and the internal temperature reaches 165°F (74°C).
5. Serve with extra BBQ sauce on the side.

Caramelized Onion BBQ Beef Burgers

Ingredients

- 1 lb ground beef
- 1/4 cup BBQ sauce
- 1 large onion, sliced
- 1 tablespoon olive oil
- 1 tablespoon brown sugar
- Salt and pepper to taste
- 4 burger buns

Instructions

1. In a pan, heat olive oil over medium heat. Add onions and cook, stirring frequently, for 10 minutes until softened.
2. Sprinkle brown sugar over onions and cook for another 5 minutes, until caramelized. Set aside.
3. In a bowl, mix ground beef with BBQ sauce, salt, and pepper. Form into 4 patties.
4. Preheat grill to medium-high heat.
5. Grill beef patties for 4–5 minutes per side, until the internal temperature reaches 160°F (71°C).
6. Serve burgers on buns, topped with caramelized onions.

Grilled Eggplant and Zucchini Rolls

Ingredients

- 1 large eggplant, sliced lengthwise into 1/4-inch thick strips
- 1 zucchini, sliced lengthwise into 1/4-inch thick strips
- 2 tablespoons olive oil
- 1 tablespoon balsamic vinegar
- Salt and pepper to taste
- 1/4 cup fresh basil, chopped
- 1/4 cup crumbled feta cheese

Instructions

1. Preheat grill to medium-high heat.
2. Brush eggplant and zucchini slices with olive oil, balsamic vinegar, salt, and pepper.
3. Grill the slices for 2–3 minutes per side, until tender.
4. Remove from grill and roll each slice around a small amount of basil and feta cheese.
5. Secure with toothpicks and serve warm.

BBQ Gingerbread-Spiced Ribs

Ingredients

- 2 racks of baby back ribs
- 1/4 cup brown sugar
- 1 tablespoon ground cinnamon
- 1 tablespoon ground ginger
- 1 teaspoon ground cloves
- 1/2 teaspoon ground nutmeg
- 1/2 cup BBQ sauce
- Salt and pepper to taste

Instructions

1. Preheat grill to medium-low heat.
2. In a small bowl, combine brown sugar, cinnamon, ginger, cloves, nutmeg, salt, and pepper.
3. Rub the spice mixture all over the ribs.
4. Grill the ribs for 2–3 hours, turning occasionally and basting with BBQ sauce every 30 minutes, until the meat is tender and caramelized.
5. Let the ribs rest for 10 minutes before slicing and serving.

Holiday Citrus BBQ Chicken Breast

Ingredients

- 4 boneless, skinless chicken breasts
- 1/4 cup orange juice
- 1/4 cup lemon juice
- 1 tablespoon olive oil
- 2 tablespoons honey
- 1 tablespoon Dijon mustard
- 1 teaspoon smoked paprika
- Salt and pepper to taste

Instructions

1. In a bowl, whisk together orange juice, lemon juice, olive oil, honey, Dijon mustard, smoked paprika, salt, and pepper.
2. Marinate chicken breasts in the citrus mixture for at least 30 minutes.
3. Preheat grill to medium heat.
4. Grill chicken breasts for 6–7 minutes per side, or until the internal temperature reaches 165°F (74°C).
5. Serve with extra citrus glaze on the side.

Cranberry Balsamic Glazed Salmon

Ingredients:

- 4 salmon fillets
- 1/2 cup fresh cranberries
- 1/4 cup balsamic vinegar
- 1 tablespoon honey
- 2 tablespoons olive oil
- 1 teaspoon fresh thyme, chopped
- Salt and pepper to taste

Instructions:

1. Preheat oven to 375°F (190°C).
2. In a small saucepan, combine cranberries, balsamic vinegar, honey, and olive oil. Cook over medium heat for 10 minutes, stirring occasionally, until the cranberries burst and the sauce thickens.
3. Season the salmon fillets with salt, pepper, and fresh thyme.
4. Place the salmon fillets on a baking sheet lined with parchment paper.
5. Brush the cranberry balsamic glaze over the salmon.
6. Bake for 15–18 minutes, or until the salmon is cooked through.
7. Serve with extra glaze drizzled on top.

Grilled Maple-Glazed Sweet Corn

Ingredients:

- 6 ears of corn, husked
- 1/4 cup maple syrup
- 2 tablespoons olive oil
- 1 tablespoon butter, melted
- 1 teaspoon smoked paprika
- Salt and pepper to taste

Instructions:

1. Preheat grill to medium-high heat.
2. In a small bowl, whisk together maple syrup, olive oil, melted butter, smoked paprika, salt, and pepper.
3. Brush the corn with the maple glaze.
4. Grill the corn for 10–12 minutes, turning occasionally, until the kernels are tender and slightly charred.
5. Brush with more glaze as it cooks for added flavor.
6. Serve warm with a sprinkle of salt.

Smoked BBQ Chestnuts (Vegan)

Ingredients:

- 2 cups chestnuts, scored
- 2 tablespoons olive oil
- 1 tablespoon soy sauce
- 1 teaspoon smoked paprika
- 1/2 teaspoon garlic powder
- Salt and pepper to taste

Instructions:

1. Preheat smoker to 225°F (107°C).
2. In a bowl, combine olive oil, soy sauce, smoked paprika, garlic powder, salt, and pepper.
3. Toss the chestnuts in the marinade, ensuring they're evenly coated.
4. Place the chestnuts on the smoker tray or a grilling basket.
5. Smoke for 45–60 minutes, turning occasionally, until tender and slightly smoky.
6. Serve warm as a savory snack or side dish.

Grilled Rosemary Lamb Kebabs

Ingredients:

- 1 lb lamb, cut into 1-inch cubes
- 2 tablespoons fresh rosemary, chopped
- 2 tablespoons olive oil
- 2 cloves garlic, minced
- 1 tablespoon lemon juice
- Salt and pepper to taste

Instructions:

1. Preheat grill to medium-high heat.
2. In a bowl, combine lamb cubes, rosemary, olive oil, garlic, lemon juice, salt, and pepper. Toss to coat and let marinate for at least 30 minutes.
3. Thread the lamb cubes onto skewers.
4. Grill the kebabs for 4–5 minutes per side for medium-rare, or longer for your desired doneness.
5. Remove from skewers and serve hot with a side of your favorite dipping sauce.

Sweet Holiday BBQ Brisket Sandwiches

Ingredients:

- 2 lbs beef brisket
- 1/4 cup brown sugar
- 1/4 cup apple cider vinegar
- 1/4 cup BBQ sauce
- 2 tablespoons Dijon mustard
- 1 teaspoon smoked paprika
- 1/2 teaspoon ground cinnamon
- Salt and pepper to taste
- 6 sandwich buns
- Coleslaw, for serving (optional)

Instructions:

1. Preheat oven to 300°F (150°C).
2. In a bowl, mix brown sugar, apple cider vinegar, BBQ sauce, Dijon mustard, smoked paprika, cinnamon, salt, and pepper.
3. Rub the brisket with the seasoning mixture and place it in a roasting pan.
4. Cover the pan with foil and cook for 4–5 hours, or until the brisket is tender and easily shreds.
5. Remove the brisket from the oven and let it rest for 10 minutes before shredding with two forks.
6. Serve the shredded brisket on sandwich buns, topped with coleslaw if desired.

Grilled Pear and Walnut Salad

Ingredients:

- 2 ripe pears, sliced
- 1 tablespoon olive oil
- 1/4 cup crumbled blue cheese
- 1/2 cup toasted walnuts
- 4 cups mixed greens (arugula, spinach, or lettuce)
- 2 tablespoons balsamic vinaigrette
- Salt and pepper to taste

Instructions:

1. Preheat the grill to medium heat.
2. Brush the pear slices with olive oil and season with a pinch of salt and pepper.
3. Grill the pear slices for 2-3 minutes per side, until slightly charred and tender.
4. In a large bowl, combine the grilled pears, mixed greens, blue cheese, and toasted walnuts.
5. Drizzle with balsamic vinaigrette and toss gently to combine.
6. Serve immediately as a refreshing starter or side dish.

Cinnamon BBQ Pork Chops

Ingredients:

- 4 bone-in pork chops
- 2 tablespoons olive oil
- 1 tablespoon cinnamon
- 1 teaspoon smoked paprika
- 1 teaspoon garlic powder
- 1/2 teaspoon cumin
- 1/4 teaspoon cayenne pepper
- Salt and pepper to taste
- 1/4 cup BBQ sauce

Instructions:

1. Preheat grill to medium-high heat.
2. In a small bowl, mix together the olive oil, cinnamon, smoked paprika, garlic powder, cumin, cayenne pepper, salt, and pepper.
3. Rub the spice mixture evenly over the pork chops.
4. Grill the pork chops for 5-7 minutes per side, until cooked through and the internal temperature reaches 145°F (63°C).
5. During the last few minutes of grilling, brush with BBQ sauce for a flavorful glaze.
6. Remove from the grill and let rest for 5 minutes before serving.

Pomegranate BBQ Glazed Chicken Wings

Ingredients:

- 12 chicken wings
- 1/2 cup pomegranate juice
- 1/4 cup BBQ sauce
- 2 tablespoons honey
- 1 tablespoon soy sauce
- 1 teaspoon garlic powder
- 1 teaspoon ground ginger
- Salt and pepper to taste

Instructions:

1. Preheat grill to medium heat.
2. In a saucepan, combine pomegranate juice, BBQ sauce, honey, soy sauce, garlic powder, and ground ginger. Simmer over medium heat for 10 minutes until the sauce thickens.
3. Season the chicken wings with salt and pepper.
4. Grill the wings for 20-25 minutes, turning occasionally, until crispy and cooked through.
5. During the last few minutes, brush the wings with the pomegranate BBQ glaze and continue grilling.
6. Serve the wings with extra glaze on the side.

Grilled Holiday Shrimp Skewers

Ingredients:

- 1 lb large shrimp, peeled and deveined
- 2 tablespoons olive oil
- 1 tablespoon lemon juice
- 1 teaspoon smoked paprika
- 1/2 teaspoon garlic powder
- Salt and pepper to taste
- 8 wooden skewers, soaked in water for 30 minutes

Instructions:

1. Preheat the grill to medium-high heat.
2. In a bowl, combine olive oil, lemon juice, smoked paprika, garlic powder, salt, and pepper.
3. Toss the shrimp in the marinade and let sit for 15-20 minutes.
4. Thread the shrimp onto the soaked skewers.
5. Grill the shrimp for 2-3 minutes per side until pink and opaque.
6. Serve with lemon wedges and fresh herbs for garnish.

Spiced BBQ Holiday Meatloaf

Ingredients:

- 1 lb ground beef
- 1/2 lb ground pork
- 1/2 cup breadcrumbs
- 1/4 cup grated parmesan cheese
- 1 egg
- 1/4 cup milk
- 1/4 cup BBQ sauce
- 1 teaspoon ground cumin
- 1 teaspoon ground cinnamon
- 1 teaspoon smoked paprika
- 1/2 teaspoon garlic powder
- Salt and pepper to taste

Instructions:

1. Preheat grill to medium heat and set up for indirect grilling.
2. In a large bowl, combine ground beef, ground pork, breadcrumbs, parmesan cheese, egg, milk, BBQ sauce, cumin, cinnamon, smoked paprika, garlic powder, salt, and pepper.
3. Shape the mixture into a loaf and place it on a piece of aluminum foil.
4. Grill the meatloaf indirectly for 45-60 minutes, or until the internal temperature reaches 160°F (71°C).
5. Brush with additional BBQ sauce during the last 10 minutes of cooking.
6. Let the meatloaf rest for 10 minutes before slicing and serving.

Hickory-Smoked BBQ Tofu (Vegan)

Ingredients:

- 1 block firm tofu, pressed and cut into 1-inch slices
- 2 tablespoons olive oil
- 1/4 cup BBQ sauce
- 1 tablespoon liquid smoke
- 1 teaspoon smoked paprika
- Salt and pepper to taste

Instructions:

1. Preheat smoker to 225°F (107°C).
2. In a bowl, mix olive oil, BBQ sauce, liquid smoke, smoked paprika, salt, and pepper.
3. Brush the tofu slices with the marinade on both sides.
4. Place the tofu slices on the smoker rack and smoke for 30-40 minutes, flipping halfway through.
5. Serve the smoked tofu on a bun with your favorite vegan condiments or alongside grilled vegetables for a complete meal.

www.ingramcontent.com/pod-product-compliance
Lightning Source LLC
LaVergne TN
LVHW061953070526
838199LV00060B/4094